What people are saying about Janell Billiot, author of Navigating the American Dream*!*

"My husband and I had the pleasure of working with Janell last year to buy our first home. She was the constant warmth and sparkle through the whole process. It seemed we had several curve balls come our way over the months, but she never gave up! She was open and honest about everything, and really went above and beyond to get us into our new home. She maintains professionalism, while still having a sense of humor along the way. I feel as though she is more than our Realtor, she has become our friend. Going forward, I wouldn't have anyone else by my side."
    Jessica & Ryan Stewart

"Janell is always so kind and honest and determined to find you exactly what you want! If she feels it's not what your family needs she will never try to persuade you to buy it just to make a sale. We wouldn't work with anyone else. She helped us with our first house and she will be who we call in the future. Very pleased!"
    Ashley & Cody Mason

Navigating the American Dream

What every buyer should know about purchasing a home in South Mississippi

Janell Billiot
GRI, SFR, BROKER ASSOCIATE

REALTOR® OF THE YEAR 2011
Pearl River County Board of REALTORS®

Copyright © 2018 Janell Billiot

All rights reserved. No part of this book may be reproduced or transmitted in any form or by any means, electronic or mechanical, including photocopying, recording, or by any information storage and retrieval system, without permission in writing from the author.

Printed in the United States of America

Billiot, Janell Hoffman / Navigating the American Dream: What every homebuyer should know about purchasing a Home in South Mississippi

ISBN: 978-1985648609

1. Real Estate   2. Sales   3. Mississippi

Published by JHB Media

Cover Design: Brett Miller/HoopJumper.com
Edited by Debbie Bourgeois – debbiebourgeois@cox.net
Photo of Janell Billiot by Kristi Harris Photography
Other Photos: © SeanPavonePhoto/Adobe Stock, Sepavone/Deposit Photos, Timurlaykov/Deposit Photos

JanellBilliot.net
MississippiRealEstateNow.com
MakeMississippiHome.com

First Edition: March 2018

This book is dedicated to

*My dearest friend Debbie Bourgeois
for her forever encouraging words
day-in and day-out*

*My REALTOR® friends who strive to exhibit
on-going professionalism in order to set
high industry standards*

*Cheri Alguire & Brett Miller for their
selfless never-ending support, friendship
and devotion to never quitting*

*And most of all, to anyone willing to
capture the American dream of
owning your own home.*

~

*A very special thanks to my good friend and
expert loan consultant Michelle McBride
for her contributions to this book.*

Table of Contents

What people are saying about Janell Billiot, author of Navigating the American Dream! 1

Introduction 1

Reviewing your financial position and setting a budget - How this will assist you in your home ownership goals? ..3

Understanding the home buying process – What to consider? 7

Selecting a local area lender – What should you think about when you are preparing to meet with a lender? 9

Selecting a local area real estate agent – Why is it important to interview agents? 12

Pre-Approval Letter and Pre-Approved – What's the difference? 17

Narrowing the location and choosing properties that fit your criteria – Where do you want to live and what do you want in a home? 19

Buyer's choice – How do I know which is the best property for me? 21

Property disclosures and comparable sales – Why should I care? 23

Submitting the offer and deposit – What does it take to get "under contract"? 25

Under Contract – What's next? 29

Due Diligence Period – Do I have to pay for an appraisal and home inspection? 33

Closing Process – What to expect? 37

The Walk-Through – I've already seen the house, can I just skip it? 39

Final Checklist – How do I prepare for move day? 41

Closing Day - What to expect? 43

Congratulations! - Attaining the Desired Goal of Home Ownership 45

Conclusion 47

About the Author, Janell Billiot 49

Contact Information 51

Introduction

In my first short book "Make Mississippi Home – Selling Your Home in South Mississippi and Maximizing Your Real Estate Investment" I outlined informative tidbits for sellers to prepare their home for sale in the market place and what to expect throughout the entire process.

This second book is written to educate buyers who may be interested in home ownership. There are so many factors that come together in order to purchase a home and it is my desire to outline the steps to home ownership as simply as possible. Yes, it can get confusing. However, with the proper guidance from your lender and real estate agent, you can and will navigate throughout the tumultuous puzzle of home buying!

Included within this book is advice from a South Mississippi local area lender, Michelle McBride. Her opinion is valued highly and her experience, knowledge and client service is top notch! I've had the pleasure of not only developing a business relationship with Michelle but through the years am glad to call her a friend. She is truly a gem!

Breathe! Breathe deeply! And before you know it, you will be a new homeowner enjoying all the benefits of owning your home.

Welcome to the American Dream!

Reviewing your financial position and setting a budget - How this will assist you in your home ownership goals?

Considering buying a home for the first time seems to be an overwhelming task. Where should we start? This is the first question that arises when you are considering a home purchase and rightfully so.

When you do not know where to start, typically the potential buyer decides to start driving around to view homes, search out locations that may be of interest, scope out all the school locations and then automatically begin calling agents to start viewing homes that may be of interest. While some of these intentions are noteworthy, there is a time-proven method to beginning a search to find your dream home and successfully accomplish your goals.

Homework first! The absolute first steps you should take to start the process are to review your finances. BEFORE you begin looking for your "Dream Home" you should find out what you can afford and what price you can handle for monthly payments. Nothing is more disappointing than finding your dream home and then finding out later that you are over budget and cannot afford it.

Buying a home is a long-term commitment and one that should not be taken lightly. Depending on your personal circumstances, several factors should be considered to decide whether it is a good time for you to buy. Some factors may include your current job status, job relocation, marital status, children, and schools. You get the idea.

If you plan on staying in the area and are not relocating then this may be a good time for you to purchase a home. If you are unsure what the near future may hold, it may be best to put off homeownership at this time.

Having a checking or savings account with some reserves in it will afford you the opportunity to show stability to the lender and allow you a cushion for those rainy days that certainly will come. If you do not currently have the ability to build a savings account, you may be better off waiting.

Another consideration is available cash towards a down payment, closing costs and other miscellaneous expenses that may arise. First look at your savings. A good rule of thumb is to have three to six months of living expenses in savings. Figure out how much is left over in your savings that could be applied to your down payment.

Next thing is to review exactly how much you are spending every month and where it's going. This will tell you how much you can allocate to your mortgage payment. Take into account your monthly expenses such as utilities, food, car payments and maintenance, clothing, kids' activities, entertainment, savings and miscellaneous items.

This review will help you figure out where your mortgage payment fits into your budget. Most couples believe that rental payments give them a good idea of what they can or cannot afford but should still take into consideration home maintenance and repairs that will now be their responsibility as a new homeowner.

These are all things that you will want to consider to help determine whether buying a house is the right move for you at this time. Once you have determined your financial position the next question would logically be – "How much money do we qualify for in order to purchase a home?"

This is a question that all buyers wonder about at the beginning of their journey to purchase a home. So another important first step is to meet with a reputable mortgage lender or banker (maybe even a few) who can review your financial position and work with you to find out how much house you can afford and how much cash you'll need to close.

A mortgage lender will sit down and review all of your personal financial information and begin the process to assist you. This process is involved and working with an experienced lender is a good place to start. Seeking wise counsel with a reputable lender to review your financial position will not only give you an idea of what price range you can afford, but will save you time and energy.

A lender will assess your credit score and the amount you can qualify for on a loan. They will also discuss your assets like savings accounts, 401(k), and of course any debt, and will explain any local programs that might be available for down payment assistance. There may be first-time homebuyer programs available to you. Do a little research online regarding local or state programs. If you qualify, assistance for your down payment may be available.

While doing research online can educate you on the lending process, working with a live person locally has added benefit because they can review your situation, answer your questions and be available to walk you through the process.

There are additional fees in your monthly note and these will need to be discussed with the lender. The purchase price and the mortgage payment are just the beginning.

Don't forget homeowner's insurance, real estate taxes and PMI (private mortgage insurance required if the down payment is less than 20%), which are all included in your monthly payment.

The lender can explain in detail what the actual fees for the loan will be. Do your homework. Just because a lender states you can borrow $100,000 doesn't mean that you should. On the other hand, if you do have credit issues that need to be addressed, keep in mind that this part of the process could take several months.

The lender meeting is a critical step in the process especially because many real estate agents will not begin working with a potential buyer until they have taken the initial steps to know how much they can afford to spend. Another important point is that most sellers will not entertain any offer that is not submitted with a pre-approval letter from the lender.

Don't be bound by loyalty when seeking a pre-approval or searching for a mortgage. Shop lenders even if you only qualify for one type of loan.

Fees can be surprisingly varied from one lender to another. For example, an FHA loan may have different fees depending on if you're applying for the loan through a local bank, credit union, mortgage banker, large bank or mortgage broker.

And…even consider a back-up lender. Keep in mind that the lender is the most important person to execute closing the loan on time.

Understanding the home buying process – What to consider?

This is a time you want to avoid spending any of your savings account or cash. When you begin to look at houses, focus on the right things.

Try not to focus on cosmetic things such as paint colors, dirty carpet, or current appliances. Focus instead on the bones of the home. Get a sense of the size of the home while you are there - the floor plan, the number of bedrooms and baths, the yard, the roof. You get the idea.

Depending on the floor plan a house can feel very small or quite the opposite – very spacious. Spaciousness can be perceived differently depending on room size and even ceiling height. Most important is how the home feels. Can you picture yourself living there? Don't rush…you will know when you find your perfect home.

Keep in mind the location is something you will not be able to change. Flooring, granite countertops and stainless-steel appliances are an easy fix at a later date. Be sure to check out the exterior of the home as well, photos of a home can be deceiving. Check out the neighborhood. School districts can affect the price of a home. This is very important too especially for re-sale value.

Also, buy somewhere you would like to live for at least five years. You won't have much equity in your home for a few years. You may have to live in your home three of the five years to avoid capital gains taxes (consult with your tax advisor for details).

If the home is located in a subdivision you will want to find out if there are any restrictive covenants that affect the property. If there is a subdivision civic association, you should be aware of their current rules and regulations.

For the next forty-five to sixty days you will feel captive to the loan process. Keep in mind that it is in your best interest to NOT make any large purchases especially automobiles or anything that will change your debt to income ratio.

This is critical to the home loan process and changes in your spending habits could cause you to lose your loan qualification status and not be able to purchase your home after all.

Selecting a local area lender – What should you think about when you are preparing to meet with a lender?

This is an area that I believe would be better left to a professional in this respective field. So, I requested a local area lender, Michelle McBride, to give us her input. And, thankfully, she did! Following are some of Michelle's suggestions.

Be prepared to discuss your credit and your monthly income. Have a comfortable number in mind for a monthly payment. Have your budget ready but most important …

"Don't be married to your mortgage!"

Here are some things Michelle suggested you have understanding of when you are talking to a lender about your credit:

What is a credit score?

A credit score is a number that represents the credit worthiness of a person. This number represents a calculation used on the credit that you have.

Typically, this number is a three-digit number that can range from a 300-850. If you have a higher number score, then that usually means you have taken care of your business and are not a high user of credit.

Your credit score is the most important number you need to know and to know why it is the number it is.

Don't be fooled by the free credit monitors offered online as each credit vendor has a different approach and different models. These models are typically designed for a specific purpose. Most of those models are not the same as a financial institution uses and will usually be different, a lot different.

If you want to see your actual score go to www.freecreditreport.com and request one. You are entitled to one free report each year.

How is your credit going to be used?

Your credit score is used as an indicator on how you take care of business. It will allow the lender to see your whole financial picture.

How much credit you have, how much credit you use and how you are paying on the current credit.

We, as mortgage lenders, use your credit to determine whether we can help you get a loan and typically it helps indicate at what price it will cost you.

How many scores do you have?

You have three credit scores. There are three main repositories for the credit base. They are Equifax, Experian, and Trans Union.

When applying for a mortgage loan they typically pull what they call a "tri" merge report, which means that they pull the scores from all three repositories under one transaction.

Other companies may only pull credit from one source and some companies only report to certain bureaus. When you have this situation, there is usually a large difference in the scores due to the reporting.

Remember Credit Scores are dynamic and since creditors regularly update information they are going to change regularly.

NAVIGATING THE AMERICAN DREAM

When you are ready to be serious about house shopping find a lender you can trust and you feel like you can relate to. Get pre-qualified. Discuss all your options for a mortgage and any concerns you have about your credit. Your lender can be your best asset in helping you get your credit where it needs to be to be able to achieve that ultimate goal of home ownership.

Selecting a local area real estate agent – Why is it important to interview agents?

What should you be looking for in a real estate agent? When you decide to sell or buy your home, what do you look for in a real estate agent?

Once you know how much you can afford and the loan amount you'll qualify for, then it is time to find a real estate agent. Real estate agents do a lot of groundwork up front for you. They search the multiple listing services for homes that fit your criteria. They will contact listing agents to set up showings and they help you negotiate the purchase of your future home. They provide all of the area information that you may need in order for you to check out the area of interest to you.

What I personally would look for when choosing a real estate agent helped me to compose this list. These are just a few questions to help you arrive at a decision in order to work together with the real estate agent to start the process.

Proven track record – Does the real estate agent consistently list and sell properties?

Knowledge of the market area – Does the real estate agent have a basic knowledge of the area you are interested in?

Knowledge of the industry - Does the real estate agent understand the process and have a basic knowledge of the process?

Dependability – Is the real estate agent dependable and exhibits follow through and follow up?

Ethical – Does the real estate agent exhibit professionalism and ethics?

Punctuality – Is the real estate agent on time? There may be instances where traffic or a previous appointment may run longer than expected however, for the most part, being punctual is important not only to the potential buyer but also to the seller who may be expecting you during a certain scheduled time frame.

Negotiating Skills – Does the real estate agent appear to have a sense of negotiating skills? This will come into play once you have found a home that is of interest to you to submit an offer on. The difference between deals that close and deals that don't are the professionals involved.

Communication Skills - Does the real estate agent communicate well?

Do you believe as a buyer that the real estate agent will be a good fit to work with you throughout the process? You want to make sure you find a real estate agent who will move quickly when a new listing goes on the market, as well as an agent who will advise you honestly on preparing your offer. It takes teamwork.

Full time real estate agent – Is the real estate agent dedicated to the profession and are they a full time real estate agent?

Trust – Do you trust the real estate agent that you have chosen to work with? This is important to consider because the agent you choose to work with will also work with you to negotiate the purchase of your home.

How do real estate agents get paid?

Real estate agents are typically paid by the seller as part of the listing agreement between the seller and the listing brokerage that is hired to list their property. Agents are paid through the Multiple Listing Service participation.

Why is it important to select the right real estate agent for you?

Often the Buyer will call the first real estate agent they come across to show them a property, whereas they should really take the time to interview multiple real estate agents from both the same and different companies.

It is a good practice to interview at least three real estate agents, weigh the differences, and then choose the one that has the qualities you are looking for. It's important to find a good fit with an agent who will work with you through the sales process and who you feel you can trust.

Also, make sure you confirm that they are 'full-time' agents. Not that part-time agents are necessarily less capable; but typically, when someone is full time they are more readily available to assist a client or potential customer. Also, full-time agents are usually more experienced.

And speaking of being readily available, it is absolutely imperative that you find an agent who will return your phone calls in a timely manner. Sometimes the agent may be showing a property or working with another client, but these days, a text is an easy acknowledgement.

Personally, I do not like to answer my phone if I am with another client, but I always return my calls the same business day, and I make some sort of contact with my client or potential customer as soon as time permits.

The next thing to consider is the experience that an agent offers. Granted, we all start somewhere, but real estate can be complicated and there's a lot to learn.

Over the years, one gains a lot of valuable knowledge and experience from different scenarios, and experience gives one the confidence to make the tough decisions.

Take the time to find an agent who you can both work and communicate with. After all, you are about to make a big decision and you should be as informed as possible.

Pre-Approval Letter and Pre-Approved – What's the difference?

Your lender will review this process with you. There is a difference in having a pre-approval letter, which is a statement of creditworthiness for general credit approval, and being pre-approved for a loan, which is a specific commitment for a maximum loan amount. Pre-approval for a loan will allow you to be ready to buy a home. It also gives you a good idea on how much money a bank or lender is willing to lend you.

The pre-approval process will begin with the information you provide to the mortgage lender. Once you provide all of the documents necessary for the lender to submit the package to the underwriter for verification of your information, the underwriting process then begins.

Sometimes in this process the underwriter may require further verification of personal information. It is in your best interest to continue to work with your lender to provide all of the information that the underwriter may require as quickly as possible in order to finalize the loan.

Once the underwriter completes this process, you will have the final loan approval and will then be able to move forward to a closing date.

When this step is achieved, the lender will then forward a title search request to the escrow agent or closing attorney. This is a very important step as the property has to be free and clear of any title issues prior to the transfer of the property to the new owner.

Narrowing the location and choosing properties that fit your criteria – Where do you want to live and what do you want in a home?

Once you are in the market for a home, it is best to consider driving around the area that may be of interest to you. Visit your favorite neighborhoods at different times. Most neighborhoods are quiet during the week.

Consider checking out the area on a Saturday or even Saturday night. It would be good to check out the neighborhood to see if there is anything out of the ordinary that may not be likeable to you. Talk to the neighbors.

Ask about the neighborhood and even about the house you are considering. The neighbors will know just about everything you would want to know. All joking aside, neighbors know and will tell you everything!

While you are searching for your ideal property – choosing a preferred area involves questions like commute time, distance to schools and shopping, and kid's activities available. These are all important factors to be considered in the criteria that you establish for your home search.

Narrowing down the location that best suits your family can save you time, money, and frustration. Your real estate agent will assist you and provide additional information for you to make an informed decision. This is an important process, which will save valuable time in reaching your goal. Working together with your real estate agent is an important part of this process.

How many homes should I view at a time?

It's important to select the homes of interest and begin to narrow down the search. This is an important process in the overall scheme of searching for a home. Depending on location and proximity of where the homes to be viewed are located, drive time is added to the equation.

After viewing about 3 homes, the homes will begin to blend together and it may get difficult to remember all of the details. It's good to have some sort of checklist when viewing the home. This list will trigger your mind when you are reviewing the homes that you viewed that day.

Practical tips to begin searching for your first home – Make a list of your must haves and a list of your wants or desires such as:

Land - How much acreage do you want?

Location – Where do we want to live?

Size - Consider the size of the home that you may want. A good size home for a small family is about 1600 to 1800 square feet and typically includes three bedrooms and two full baths.

Schools – Research information about the area schools which you can find online through the local education system.

Parks/Recreation – Are there local parks or community activities to participate in?

Shopping/Restaurants – What is the proximity to the nearest stores and restaurants and what are the alternatives?

Buyer's choice – How do I know which is the best property for me?

Your real estate agent will assist you in your search based upon your criteria for homes of interest. Once you know the price range that you are in, your real estate agent will provide you with a list of homes currently on the market for viewing with your criteria and within your price range.

Properties are listed on the market daily. Depending on the location of the property, the price, and the condition, certain properties may move quickly. It is always best to select a home that not only is a good fit for your family, but also a home that is priced within your budget.

When you do view a home that you are interested in, keep in mind that if you are indecisive about an offer, that home may not be there tomorrow. You might not want to wait to put an offer in. The home may not be there in a few weeks or even days. This is why it is wise to have the pre-approval letter in hand so that when you find your dream home you can move forward immediately with making an offer.

Homes that are priced properly and homes that are in good condition will tend to move quicker. So, being quick to decide will benefit you greatly by not missing out on the home and if you are able to avoid a bidding war in a possible multiple offer situation.

Property disclosures and comparable sales – Why should I care?

Property disclosures are forms that the seller of the property will fill out to disclose any issues with the property. This form is detailed and requests the seller to indicate information regarding their property that is on the market for sale. This form is very important and follows the sale of the property for its lifetime.

The form should be reviewed prior to an offer being submitted by the buyers. While the sellers indicate what they know about their property, there may also be items in need of repair that the sellers are unaware of. This is where the importance of a home inspection report comes into play. NEVER skip the home inspection.

Comparable sales are used to compare what has sold in the area to give you an idea of the market. This will help you to know if you are submitting an offer that it is competitive with the current market. Comparable sales are typically chosen within a six-month retroactive sales period.

Submitting the offer and deposit – What does it take to get "under contract"?

The purchase offer process begins once you have counseled with your real estate agent and have decided to submit an offer. There is a period of time that is given to the listing agent to present the offer to the seller/owner of the property. Typically, twenty-four to forty-eight hours is the turn-around time frame, and in instances of holidays or weekends additional time may be given to the seller to respond.

A purchase offer is typically contingent on a satisfactory home inspection, borrower loan approval, and receiving a professional appraisal that is equal to or greater than the purchase price.

What to expect when you are under contract:

Once the offer has been presented to the seller, there are three possibilities that may happen:

1. The seller may accept the offer as written;

2. The seller may counter the offer; or

3. The seller may reject the offer in its entirety.

Let's review these options in the order outlined above.

Should the seller accept the offer that was originally submitted, the seller will then sign and date the document indicating their agreement to the terms. The listing agent will then contact the buyer's agent (your real estate agent) and inform the agent their offer was accepted. Your real estate agent should contact you to advise you that your offer was accepted. Once your real estate agent receives the signed offer back from the listing agent, they will provide a copy of the document to you via email, fax, hand delivery, or whatever means is agreeable to you. When the buyer or buyer's signs the acceptance, the offer with all of the required signatures now becomes a valid purchase agreement contract. At this point, the property is now considered "under contract".

Alternatively, should the seller not agree with the offer as submitted, they might counter your offer. What this means is that some of the original terms you asked for may not be agreeable to the seller for whatever reasons they have. For example, it could be price. Maybe the seller believes your initial offering price on the home was priced too low and they want to counter your offer with a higher price.

Another example is, if you asked for assistance with closing costs, the seller may not be in a position to or willing to assist you with closing costs but may be willing to split the closing costs with you – this could be a counter offer by the seller.

Whatever the reasons, these are negotiations that your real estate agent will assist you with during the offer process. This may very well continue back and forth for some time until an agreement is reached between all of the parties. A great real estate agent is familiar with the counter offer process and will advise you how to respond.

Should the Seller respond with a rejection of your offer in its entirety, some things to consider may be:

Did we submit a lower priced offer on the home against the suggestion of our real estate agent, which may have insulted the seller?

Did we request ALL or just some of the anticipated closing costs?

Were we considerate of any time constraints that we asked of the sellers?

While most real estate agents will advise their seller to work with the offer presented, there may be times where the seller will out right reject an offer. (Keep in mind that real estate agents DO NOT make the seller's decisions for them, they only convey the intent between the parties.) If this happens, your real estate agent would then advise you of your options.

My personal suggestion would be to start over with a clean offer. Maybe consider making a higher initial offer, or asking for less assistance with closing costs, or whatever may make your offer more appealing to the seller. While submitting a letter to the seller outlining your intent of purchasing their home is a great idea, this typically has not been practiced in our local market area as of yet.

Under Contract – What's next?

Once the offer has been presented and the seller reviews the offer, they have the option of accepting the offer as written, countering the offer that you presented or the option to reject the offer in its entirety.

If the seller agrees to the offer the seller will sign the offer, the listing agent will notify the buyer's agent, and the offer will be forwarded back to the buyer's agent for the buyer's acceptance signature. When all parties have accepted the offer and the last acceptance signature is signed, the offer then becomes a valid purchase agreement contract and the property is considered "under contract" once it is fully signed and the earnest money deposit is made.

The earnest money deposit is simply a good faith deposit made by the buyer towards the purchase of their new home. Typically, their check is deposited into either the listing or selling brokerage non-interest-bearing escrow account, depending on the terms of the listing agreement.

Depending on the terms of the purchase agreement contract, the earnest money deposit can sometimes be non-refundable if the buyer defaults on their agreement to purchase the property. A competent real estate agent will guide you along the way in order to have a smooth transaction and to avoid any reasons why you, as the buyer, could possibly default on the contract.

At closing, the seller's or buyer's real estate agent will typically bring the earnest money deposit check to the escrow agent or closing attorney to be applied as a credit towards your purchase price on the closing settlement statement.

Once the property is under contract the due diligence period begins. The next step in the process would be the home inspection, which is typically performed within ten business days from the date of the accepted contract.

NEVER skip the Home Inspection!

Once your offer has been accepted and is now under contract, the next step is the home inspection. There are several reasons why the buyer should never skip the home inspection.

Typically, the buyer pays for the home inspection. This is one of the initial expenses the buyer is encouraged to incur. This is an educational process about the home and will reveal to you a detailed overview of the home's condition. This inspection is normally completed within ten business days of the accepted contract and is completed by a licensed Mississippi home inspector.

While the seller has provided a property disclosure form to you regarding information they know about their property, there may be additional items revealed in the inspection report that the seller may not be aware of. The seller may be responsible for all or some of the repairs, depending on what was negotiated in the contract.

The bottom line is that a home purchase is a big financial decision. It is in your best interest to find out from a licensed Mississippi home inspector exactly what you are considering to purchase so you can make an informed decision.

This inspection report will give you additional information about the home either revealing items of concern that may need to be addressed or in some cases, items that may need repair. These revelations are shared with the seller.

Reviewing the home inspection report with the inspector will give you peace of mind. If only minor repairs are needed, sometimes the buyers will assume the repairs.

If major repairs are indicated on the report, your real estate agent can address the concerned items with the listing agent after providing a copy of the home inspection report to the seller. There may be further negotiations required at this time depending on the report.

What you don't want to happen is to forego the inspection and later discover costly repairs are needed causing you to have to take on a financial burden that you were not prepared for in the home buying process.

Due Diligence Period – Do I have to pay for an appraisal and home inspection?

Typically, once the contract is accepted there is a ten (10) day inspection or "due diligence" period for the buyer to investigate the property.

The first step is the home inspection, which allows for inspection of the home and outlines a written report of the condition of the property that you are considering for purchase. Also, the due diligence can include other items of importance such as a title review, survey review, well inspections, termite inspections…etc.

Once the home inspection report has been accepted and you agree to move forward, your real estate agent will advise the listing agent in writing that you are moving forward with the purchase of the home.

At this time you will notify your lender that you are moving forward with your purchase and the lender will require you to provide a check for a professional appraisal of the property.

The appraisal fee typically ranges from $350.00 to $600.00. Once the lender has your check in hand, they will order the appraisal.

The appraiser is selected from a rotation pool of appraisers from the lender's approved list, and the real estate agents have no say-so as to which appraiser will appraise the property. The appraiser will typically contact the listing agent for access to the property.

The appraisal process will take 7 to 10 days for the appraiser to complete their report and return it to the lender. This report will select comparable sales from the area within the past six (6) months (or more in some instances depending on the property) and will provide the lender with the necessary information required by their underwriter to approve your loan. You, as the homebuyer, will receive a copy of the appraisal for your review.

Real estate agents can provide relevant data and other information to an appraiser that enables the appraiser to render an independent, impartial and objective opinion of value.

However, there are strict guidelines for real estate agents to adhere to in that regard. The lender will advise you of the status of the appraisal and once received, will provide a copy of the appraisal report to you.

The buyer's and seller's real estate agent will not be provided with a copy of the report and will only be informed if the appraisal met the contract sales price or not.

For a maximum loan to value home loan, the lender will not loan money to the buyer unless the appraised value meets or exceeds the contract sales price.

There are instances when an appraisal may not meet the purchase contract sales price and your real estate agent will be notified (usually by you, the buyer). In those cases, your real estate agent will notify the listing agent so that the listing agent can discuss the appraisal situation with the seller. The buyer can provide the appraiser's letter with the appraised value to the seller.

Note that the buyer has the full rights to their appraisal report and may choose to share the report with their agent, though not required. In certain circumstances, it may be necessary in order to justify a reduction in sales price if property did not meet purchase amount.

Unless the buyer has the additional funds to put up (and most do not), the situation here becomes that of the lending institution not being willing to loan you, the buyer, more money than the appraised value of the home.

Another solution is if the seller will agree to reduce the sales price to move forward with the sale of their home based upon the appraisal in hand and amend the contract sales price to reflect the appraised value.

ALL parties will have to agree at this point whether to move forward or not.

Of course, keep in mind that the real estate agents involved will direct you through the process. The good news here is that typically people are more than willing to work these types of issues to mutually benefit the parties.

Closing Process – What to expect?

What is a reasonable time frame to finalize the sale of your home?

A reasonable time frame for a home closing is typically thirty to sixty days after the property is under contract provided the lender has all of your pertinent information in a timely manner in the beginning of the process.

This is important so that when the loan processor begins their process of reviewing the file ALL of the criteria is met. Underwriters do not like to touch the file numerous times.

To avoid this, it is best to provide everything that your lender requests in the beginning so as to avoid delays on the backside of the process as you near your final steps in the approval process.

Once the underwriter has reviewed your loan approval file and all conditions required have been met, the file will be cleared to close. The lender will forward a document closing package to the escrow agent or attorney to schedule the closing date.

Some local lenders can actually close within thirty days provided you stay on top of providing whatever paperwork or additional information the lender requests.

The Walk-Through – I've already seen the house, can I just skip it?

The walk-through is usually done a few days before or in some instances even on the day of closing. This very important step allows the buyer to walk through and view the property PRIOR to closing and to verify that the property is in the same condition as the day the initial offer was written.

This step allows you the opportunity to be satisfied with your purchase and also to verify that any agreed upon repairs are completed to your satisfaction and any other agreed upon terms are met.

If, for whatever reason, you are not satisfied with the property, you can elect to postpone the closing until you are satisfied with what was agreed to by the seller to be provided PRIOR to the scheduled closing.

The final walk through is imperative for the buyer to do because once you sign the act of sale document at closing, you are indicating that you accept that the agreed upon terms regarding the condition of the property have been met to your satisfaction.

Final Checklist –
How do I prepare for move day?

While you are in the process of packing and moving all of your belongings, don't forget that when you move all of your information moves too.

A good place to start is with your local post office, which provides a packet for you to fill out notification of a change in your mailing address.

Notify your monthly bills, credit card companies, auto insurance, doctors, vets and even family of your new address. This will save you time prior to your move day.

Coordinate setting up your utilities at the new house so that you will have utilities on when move in day arrives. Sellers will normally allow the new buyer time to transfer utilities into their name, eliminating the need for the buyer taking additional time from work to handle this detail once the closing has been completed.

You will be anxious and excited to move into your new home so a little preparation beforehand will save you time and bring you peace on the big move in day!

Here is a checklist that may be of help to you:

6 Weeks	Start decluttering
4 Weeks	Start packing the items you want Sell or donate any items you don't want
2 Weeks	Work on change of address with all of your bills, doctors, insurance company, utilities, etc.
1 Week	Buy only enough food for the remaining days at your current home
The Day Before Moving	Finish packing
Moving Day	Arrive at the closing on time!

Closing Day - What to expect?

On closing day, be prepared to be at the attorney or escrow agent's office for at least one hour in order to go over the sale and lender documents for signature.

The lender will make every effort to participate in the closing day by being present to assist you with any questions or concerns you may have regarding the financial portion of the closing.

The closing can be overwhelming, as it seems that the stack of documents to be signed never ends. Don't panic. The attorney or escrow agent is familiar with these documents and will make the process seem effortless.

Once the documents are signed, the attorney will disburse the proceeds to the seller (if any), the seller will provide house keys and garage door openers to the buyer and you are now a proud homeowner.

Finally, you thought you'd never get here! You can now take possession of your new home.

Congratulations! - Attaining the Desired Goal of Home Ownership

Now that the keys are in your hand you are now the proud owner of your new home! This is an exciting time and also the beginning of the move.

Keep in mind that your new home will provide you many years of warmth and security. Enjoy it to the fullest as you settle in and make the house "your home"!

Your REALTOR® is just a phone call away should you require any assistance.

Conclusion

This was a pleasure to write this second book!

My first book was an Amazon Best Seller last year (2017) thanks to wonderful uplifting mentors that I am fortunate to call "Friends" – Cheri Alguire & Brett Miller.

Make Mississippi Home: Selling Your Home in South Mississippi and Maximizing Your Real Estate Investment.

There is so much information to share. My hope is that you will have a reference of information at your fingertips not only to help you purchase a home but to share with anyone you may know who is considering buying a home. Please share this information with them as a start to their home ownership goals.

I believe the information is useful and will provide direction to answer questions one may wonder about.

Find the appropriate professionals to assist you along the way and you will successfully attain your goal of home ownership.

If you are ever in South Mississippi, drop me a line if you are in the market for real estate! It would be my pleasure to assist you!

About the Author, Janell Billiot

Janell Billiot is a seasoned Real Estate Agent and is a member of the National Association of REALTORS® and the Mississippi Association of REALTORS®.

Janell is a Primary Member of the Gulf Coast Association of REALTORS® and a Secondary Member of the Pearl River Board of REALTORS®® in Mississippi.

A consistent Multi-Million Dollar Producer, Janell was named 2011 REALTOR® OF THE YEAR for the Pearl River Board of REALTORS®

She received the prestigious Janie Mitchell Courage Award in 2016 for which her peers nominated her.

She has served on the Pearl River Board of REALTORS® in various positions over the years not only on Committees but also as Chairperson.

2009 Public Relations Chair Pearl River Board of REALTORS®

2009 Awards Committee

2010 Public Relations Chair of the Pearl River Board of REALTORS®

2010 & 2011 Director - Pearl River Board of REALTORS®

2011 Finance Committee

2012 - SECRETARY Board of Directors

2012 Education Committee

2013 Education Committee

JANELL BILLIOT

2013 Awards Committee

2014 Chair Finance Committee

2015 Chair Finance Committee

2015 Chair By-Laws Committee

2016 MLS Committee

Janell enjoys helping her fellow REALTORS® whenever asked and mostly enjoys helping sellers and buyers realize their real estate goals.

Additional accomplishments:

Associate Broker (since 2009)

Graduate - Real Estate Institute

Short Sale & Foreclosure (SFR) Certification

Multi-Million Dollar Producer

Lifetime Multi-Million Dollar Producer

2009 RE/MAX Executive Club

2011 & 2012 Spirit Award - Gardner REALTORS®

2011 REALTOR® of the Year for Pearl River Board of REALTORS®

Contact Information

Janell Billiot is an Associate Broker at Holliday Real Estate in Poplarville, MS

The office address is:

Holliday Real Estate
1729 South Main Street
Poplarville, MS 39470

601-795-9371 Office Phone

601-273-1778 Cell

Janell can be contacted by email at: janellhbilliot@gmail.com or through her personal website at www.MississippiRealEstateNow.com

www.ingramcontent.com/pod-product-compliance
Lightning Source LLC
Chambersburg PA
CBHW030051230526
45471CB00003B/1035